Sum of

The Killing of Uncle Sam
Rodney Howard-Browne and Paul L. Williams

Conversation Starters

By Paul Adams
Book Habits

Please Note: This is an unofficial Conversation Starters guide. If you have not yet read the original work, you can purchase the original book here.

Copyright © 2018 by BookHabits. All Rights Reserved. First Published in the United States of America 2018

We hope you enjoy this complementary guide from BookHabits. Our mission is to aid readers and reading groups with quality, thought provoking material to in the discovery and discussions on some of today's favorite books.

Disclaimer / Terms of Use: This guide is unofficial and unauthorized. It is not authorized, approved, licensed, or endorsed by the original book's author or publisher and any of their licensees or affiliates. Product names, logos, brands, and other trademarks featured or referred to within this publication are the property of their respective trademark holders and are not affiliated with BookHabits. The publisher and author make no representations or warranties with respect to the accuracy or completeness of these contents and disclaim all warranties such as warranties of fitness for a particular purpose.

No part of this publication may be reproduced or retransmitted, electronic or mechanical, without the written permission of the publisher.

Bonus Downloads
*Get Free Books with **Any Purchase** of* Conversation Starters!

Every purchase comes with a FREE download!

Add spice to any conversation
Never run out of things to say
Spend time with those you love

Get it Now

or Click Here.

Scan Your Phone

Tips for Using Conversation Starters:

EVERY GOOD BOOK CONTAINS A WORLD FAR DEEPER THAN the surface of its pages. Questions herein are designed to bring us beneath the surface of the page and invite us into the world that lives on. These questions can be used to:

- Foster a deeper understanding of the book
- Promote an atmosphere of discussion for groups
- Assist in the study of the book, either individually or corporately
- Explore unseen realms of the book as never seen before

Table of Contents

Introducing *The Killing of Uncle Sam* 6
Discussion Questions 14
Introducing the Author 35
Fireside Questions 42
Quiz Questions 53
Quiz Answers 66
Ways to Continue Your Reading 67

Introducing *The Killing of Uncle Sam*

Uncle Sam is indeed dead. His condition has been proven lifeless when then avuncular figure failed to respond during the most shocking blows this country ever had. In their book *The Killing of Uncle Sam: The Demise of the United States of America,* Rodney Howard-Brown and Paul Williams discusses the most horrendous attacks in history done in American soil and how Uncle Sam failed to respond and be revived.

The Killing of Uncle Sam captures the last two centuries of American history that the public knows little about. It examines the secret legalized system within the private central banks. This book follows the money trail as these banks have gone unchecked for decades. *The Killing of Uncle Sam* shows you the truths behind the enemies of the United States, both foreign and domestic.

Attacks on the once-powerful nation of America had become commonplace for decades. One of the first attack was on August 2, 1990. This was the day Saddam Hussein ordered a large number of Iraqi soldiers to invade Kuwait. His reason behind the invasion was relatively reasonable. While Iraq was engaging in war with Iran, Kuwait took the chance and pilfered billions of dollars from the Rumdia oil field owned by Iraq. The

Kuwaiti emir Amir Jabir al-Almad refused to absolve his debt and interest to his country. This posed no threat to United States national security, however, it risked the interests of two of the most powerful banking families.

The House of Rothschild and the House of Rockefeller feared that Hussein would invade the nearby country of Saudi Arabia and control the oil fields along the Persian Gulf. These two banking families operated Exxon and BP, two of the world's largest oil companies. In the 1930s, they were the families behind Saudi Aramco and were the largest purchasers of oil from the Middle East. Their position to purchase oil and determine its price became threatened when Hussein started the invasion in Saudi Arabia. George Schultz, CFR and the Reagan Administration has been on Iraq's side during the Iran-Iraq war. The government gave billions worth of agricultural credits and millions of dollars' worth of weapons to Saddam. These were transported through Egypt and Saudi Arabia. The goal was to end the reign of Iran's Ayatollah Khomeini.

The alliance between the American government and Hussein came to an end when a prominent CFR member became president. When Saddam Hussein has ventured into Kuwait, President George H. W. Bush decided to launch war against Iraq, an ally. Bush has extensive ties with Standard Oil. Bush was associated with a leading defense contractor, the Carlyle Group. Their customers were the government of Kuwait and the Saudi royal family, among others. Through this, Bush was wired to the Saudis, the Rockefellers and the military. The only problem left for Bush to solve was how to justify the attack of US military against Iraq. The answer came through the spread of fake news. Bush and his cabinet made up stories of Hussein ordering his soldiers to remove babies from incubators in Kuwaiti hospitals. They began to circulate stories that these babies were casted on the floor to die. These sparked the beginning of the Persian Gulf War.

Shortly after, a New York–based human rights organization called Middle East Watch sent investigators to Iraq. Their goal was to verify the stories about the Iraqi troops removing infants from incubators in Kuwaiti hospitals. There was no evidence supporting the story and no medical personnel or parent could support the stories that sparked a great war.

Apart from Bush, another American president raised false news to protect the collective interests of defense contractors, the CIA and the money cartel. From March 24 to June 10 1999, President Bill Clinton ordered the US Air Force to bomb Kosovo. They did so under the auspices of NATO. They destroyed the stronghold of Christian Serbs. Clinton justified the bombing because of the alleged genocided committed by the Serbs. They were allegedly murdering thousands of Muslim Albanians in the grounds of ethnic cleansing. The Clinton administration circulated the story that thousands of Muslim Albanian bodies were dumped in a mine in Trepca. The French gendarmerie spelunking team found no body in the mine. Some villagers said the bodies were burned but the French again found no evidence of bones, flesh or any human remains.

Barnes & Noble readers said that *The Killing of Uncle Sam* is eye-opening and "a must-read for every American citizen." Jason Monchgesang, an American reader reviewed the book and praises how it details the use of the military, media, and American money to propagate wars for personal sinister interests. He says that he is "beginning to understand the truth."

Discussion Questions

"Get Ready to Enter a New World"

Tip: Begin with questions dealing with broader issues to ensure ample time for quality discussions. Read through all discussion questions before engaging.

~~~

question 1

Rodney Howard-Brown and Paul Williams discussed the most horrendous attacks in history done in American soil and how Uncle Sam failed to respond and be revived. What is an example of horrendous attacks on American soil?

~~~

~~~

question 2

Attacks on America had become a common happening for decades. One of the first attack was on August 2, 1990. What significant event happened on this date?

~~~

~~~

question 3

Saddam Hussein ordered Iraqi soldiers to invade Kuwait. His reason behind the invation was relatively reasonable. What is Sadam Hussein's reason behind the invasion?

~~~

~~~

question 4

The Kuwaiti emir Amir Jabir al-Almad refused to absolve his debt and interest to Iraq and during the war, Kuwait pilfered billions of dollars from Iraq's Rumdia oil field. How do these events affect the United States?

~~~

~~~

question 5

During the war in the Middle East, two of the most powerful banking families were gravely affected. They controlled two of the world's largest oil companies. Who are these two powerful families?

~~~

~~~

question 6

In the 1930s, the families behind Saudi Aramco were the largest purchasers of oil from the Middle East. They purchased oil and determined its price. What are the two large American-owned oil companies in the 1930s?

~~~

~~~

question 7

George Schultz, CFR and the Reagan Administration have been aiding Iraq during the Iran-Iraq war. They gave millions of dollars' worth of weapons to Saddam Hussein. What was the collective goal of Saddam Hussein, George Schultz, CFR and the Reagan Administration?

~~~

~~~

question 8

The alliance between the American government and Hussein came to an end when a prominent CFR member became president. When Saddam Hussein has ventured into Kuwait, this president launched war against its long-time ally, Iraq. Who is this president?

~~~

~~~

question 9

During the Iran-Iraq War, the American president had extensive ties with the company Standard Oil. He was also associated with a defense contractor whose customer was the Kuwaiti government. What is the name of this leading defense contractor?

~~~

~~~

question 10

The only problem left for the president was how to justify the attack of US military against Iraq. The answer came through the spread of a false flag. What false news was spread about Saddam Hussein?

~~~

~~~

question 11

The false news that sparked the beginning of the Persian Gulf War moved a New York–based human rights organization to verify the news. They sent investigators to Iraq. What is the name of this human rights organization? What did they find out?

~~~

~~~

question 12

President Bill Clinton also raised false news to protect the collective interests of defense contractors, the CIA and the money cartel. In 1999, he ordered the US Air Force to bomb a state in Southeastern Europe. What state was bombed during Clinton's term?

~~~

~~~

question 13

Clinton justified the bombing because of the alleged genocide committed by the Serbs. The grounds was ethnic cleansing. Who was the people group that was allegedly killed by the Serbs?

~~~

~~~

question 14

The Clinton administration circulated a false story. The story goes that thousands of bodies were dumped in a mine after being massacred. What is the name of the mine where the bodies dumped?

~~~

~~~

question 15

The French gendarmerie spelunking team found no body in the mine. Some villagers said the bodies were burned so the team examined the ashes. What was the result of their investigation?

~~~

question 16

Anti-Terrorism Expert and Former CIA Officer Kevin Shipp says that this book is unquestionably "the most accurate description of the deep state shadow government." How did Williams and Howard-Browne describe the current state of the American nation?

~~~

~~~

question 17

Barnes & Noble readers said that *The Killing of Uncle Sam* is eye-opening and "a must-read for every American citizen." Why does every American citizen need to read *The Killing of Uncle Sam*?

~~~

question 18

Jason Monchgesang, an American reader reviewed the book and praised how it details the use of the military, media, and American money to propagate wars for personal sinister interests. He says that he is "beginning to understand the truth." Which is the most shocking revelation in the book?

~~~

question 19

An Amazon reader highly recommends the book as this book has provided "factual information about who is really in charge of 'the system'." According to the authors, who are the personalities that are behind the system?

~~~

~~~

question 20

Another Amazon reader says that *The Killing of Uncle Sam* is logical and is "a powerful weapon in the right hands." How can the truth be a weapon? Do you find the revelations in the book logical?

~~~

Introducing the Author

The Killing of Uncle Sam co-author Rodney Howard-Browne is an evangelist and a Charismatic Christian preacher by vocation. He serves as the senior pastor of The River at Tampa Bay. His wife Adonica Howard-Browne founded the church with him in 1996. He and his wife lead Revival Ministries International. Howard-Browne was born in South Africa. He was raised in a Pentecostal family and grew up in Eastern Cape. He met his wife in 1981. They married the same year and went together into a traveling ministry full-time. For over six years, they traveled across Africa, particularly Namibia and Zimbabwe. They preached the Gospel and in 1983, they planted a church in Northeastern Cape. They led and pastored the church for two years before Rodney Howard-Browne taught classes in a Bible School. During this time, they had three children together named Kirsten, Kelly and Kenneth. Rodney and Adonica felt the call to go to the United States of America. Rodney visited the country twice that year to preach in different churches. The whole family moved to United States in December 1987.

In 1996, Rodney and Adonica Howard-Browne started a church in Florida called The River by Tampa Bay. *Christianity Today* described Browne's ministry as passionate for evangelism and ministries of restoration. They are characteristically accompanied by the Holy Spirit through "signs and wonders". They have regular baptisms of the Holy Spirit and Fire together with miracles and physical healings. The River at Tampa Bay gave rise to the terms 'holy ghost bartender' and 'holy laughter.' Their church The River at Tampa Bay is celebrating their twenty-second year in 2018. Howard-Browne was one of seventeen pastors who visited the White House in July 2017. He was invited to pray for and lay hands on the newly elected President Donald Trump. He was accused of alleged plots against the president. Rodney Howard-Browne co-authored *The Killing of Uncle Sam* with Paul L. Williams.

Paul L. Williams is an American journalist, author and professor. He teaches humanities and philosophy at The University of Scranton and Wilkes University. Williams is raised in a Roman Catholic family. His family has Irish roots and were one of the first coal miner families in Scranton Pennsylvania. Williams earned his Bachelor's Degree in English from Wilkes University. He then earned a Master of Divinity degree from Drew University. He later received his Doctor of Philosophy degree from the same university. His doctoral dissertation topic was the moral philosophy of Peter Abelard based on Latin texts.

Williams published his first book in 1989 under Doubleday Publishing. His book was entitled

Everything You Always Wanted To Know about the Catholic Church But Were Afraid to Ask for Fear of Excommunication. Thereafter, he has written twelve books on politics, religion and history. Some of his books are *Al Qaeda: Brotherhood of Terror* and *The Life and Work of Mother Teresa* under Alpha Publishing. He then published three books under Prometheus Books entitled, *The Vatican Exposed. Money, Murder, and the Mafia*; *Al Qaeda Connection: International Terrorism, Organized Crime, and the Coming Apocalypse* and *Osama's Revenge: The Next 9/11: What the Media and the Government Haven't Told You.* His 2003 book *The Vatican Exposed*, became the subject of a Discovery Channel documentary. Booklist acclaimed this book as "a thoroughly documented and compelling challenge for reform." He additionally published two books under Prometheus Books entitled *Operation Gladio: The Unholy Alliance between the Vatican, the CIA, and the Mafia* and *The Day of Islam: The Annihilation of America and the Western World.*

Williams wrote articles for *The Wall Street Journal, National Review* and *USA Today*. In the same year, he won three first-place Keystone Press Awards in three different categories. He has regular guest appearances on news programs like MSNBS and Fox News, among others.

Bonus Downloads
*Get Free Books with **Any Purchase** of* Conversation Starters!

Every purchase comes with a FREE download!

Add spice to any conversation
Never run out of things to say
Spend time with those you love

Get it Now

or Click Here.

Scan Your Phone

Fireside Questions

"What would you do?"

Tip: These questions can be a fun exercise as it spurs creativity among the readers by allowing alternate scene endings and "if this was you" questions.

~~~

question 21

Howard-Browne encountered controversy when was invited to pray for the newly elected President Donald Trump. He was accused of alleged plot against the president. How does this controvery affect how the American audience receive his book *The Killing of Uncle Sam?*

~~~

~~~

question 22

Award-winning journalist Paul L. Williams has written books about politics, religion and government. Why is it essential for Williams to co-author the book and not just Howard-Browne?

~~~

~~~

question 23

Paul L. Williams' 2003 book *The Vatican Exposed* became the subject of a Discovery Channel documentary. Booklist acclaimed this book as "a thoroughly documented and compelling challenge for reform." What is the message of this book?

~~~

~~~

question 24

The Killing of Uncle Sam co-author Rodney Howard-Browne is an evangelist and a preacher by vocation. His church The River at Tampa Bay has been serving its people for the past 22 years. What makes Howard-Browne qualified to write *The Killing of Uncle Sam?*

~~~

question 25

Paul L. Williams' 2014 book *Operation Gladio: The Unholy Alliance between the Vatican, the CIA, and the Mafia* is praised by *The Washington Book Review*. They say that its "estimable scholarly and intellectual accomplishment which is unrivaled." What is the collective characteristic of the books written by Paul L. Williams? What is the overarching message of his books?

~~~

~~~

question 26

The American government gave millions of dollars' worth of weapons to Saddam. The goal was to end the reign of Iran's Ayatollah Khomeini. If you were the American president during this time, will you aid a foreign nation to overthrow another? Why or why not?

~~~

~~~

question 27

When Saddam Hussein ventured into Kuwait, President George H. W. Bush decided to launch war against his nation Iraq. Iraq and United States have been allies for decades until this moment. If you were Saddam Hussein, how will you respond to these attacks?

~~~

~~~

question 28

Bush and his cabinet said that Hussein ordered his soldiers to remove babies from incubators in Kuwaiti hospitals. They began to circulate stories that these babies were casted on the floor to die. If you learned that this news is fabricated, how will you view your government?

~~~

~~~

question 29

Middle East Watch sent investigators to Iraq to verify the stories about the Iraqi troops removing infants from incubators in Kuwaiti hospitals. There was no evidence and no medical personnel or parent who could support the stories. If you were part of the team of investigators, how will you react to the lack of evidence?

~~~

~~~

question 30

The Clinton administration circulated the story that thousands of Muslim Albanian bodies were dumped in a mine in Trepca. A French team found no body in the mine nor evidence of human remains in the ashes. If you were one of the villagers in Kosovo, will you hide the truth from the investigators? Why or why not?

~~~

Quiz Questions

"Ready to Announce the Winners?"

Tip: Create a leaderboard and track scores to see who gets the most correct answers. Winners required. Prizes optional.

~~~

quiz question 1

During the war in the Middle East, two of the most powerful banking families were gravely affected. They controlled two of the world's largest oil companies. Who are these two powerful families?

~~~

~~~

quiz question 2

The alliance between the American government and Hussein came to an end when a prominent CFR member became president. When Saddam Hussein has ventured into Kuwait, this president launched war against Iraq. Who is this president?

~~~

~~~

quiz question 3

During the Iran-Iraq War, the American president had associations with a defense contractor whose customer was the Kuwaiti government. What is the name of this leading defense contractor?

~~~

~~~

quiz question 4

Clinton justified the bombing of Kosovo because of the alleged genocide committed by the Serbs. Who was the people group that was allegedly killed by the Serbs?

~~~

~~~

quiz question 5

True or False: Thousands of Muslim Albanian bodies were suspected to be dumped in a mine in Trepca. A French team found body remains in the mine.

~~~

~~~

quiz question 6

True or False: Middle East Watch verified the stories about the Iraqi troops removing infants from incubators in Kuwaiti hospitals. Al Kuwait hospital doctors and nurses supported the story.

~~~

~~~

quiz question 7

True or False: In 1990, Saddam Hussein ordered Iraqi soldiers to invade Kuwait. He ordered this because Kuwait pilfered billions of dollars from an Iraqi oil field.

~~~

~~~

quiz question 8

Rodney Howard-Browne serves as the senior pastor of The River at Tampa Bay. He founded this church with his wife _____ in 1996.

~~~

~~~

quiz question 9

Paul L. Williams published _____ in 2003. This book became the subject of a Discovery Channel documentary.

~~~

~~~

quiz question 10

Paul L. Williams is an American journalist, author and professor. He teaches humanities and philosophy at The University of Scranton and _____.

~~~

~~~

quiz question 11

True or False: Paul L. Williams received his Doctor of Philosophy degree from Drew University. His doctoral dissertation topic was the moral philosophy of Julian of Norwich based on Latin texts.

~~~

~~~

quiz question 12

True or False: Howard-Browne was one of seventeen pastors who visited the White House in July 2017. He was invited to pray for and lay hands on the newly elected President Donald Trump. He was accused of alleged plots against the president.

~~~

Quiz Answers

1. The House of Rothschild and the House of Rockefeller
2. President George H.W. Bush
3. The Carlyle Group
4. Muslim Albanians
5. False
6. False
7. True
8. Adonica Howard-Browne
9. The Vatican Exposed. Money, Murder, and the Mafia
10. Wilkes University
11. False
12. True

Ways to Continue Your Reading

EVERY month, our team runs through a wide selection of books to pick the best titles for readers and reading groups, and promotes these titles to our thousands of readers – sometimes with free downloads, sale dates, and additional brochures.

Click here to sign up for these benefits.

If you have not yet read the original work or would like to read it again, you can purchase the original book here.

Bonus Downloads

*Get Free Books with **Any Purchase** of Conversation Starters!*

Every purchase comes with a FREE download!

*Add spice to any conversation
Never run out of things to say
Spend time with those you love*

Get it Now

or Click Here.

Scan Your Phone

On the Next Page...

If you found this book helpful to your discussions and rate it a 4 or 5, please write us a review on the next page.

Any length would be fine but we'd appreciate hearing you more! We'd be very encouraged.

Till next time,

BookHabits

"Loving Books is Actually a Habit"